The WIT and
BLASPHEMY
of ATHEISTS

The WIT and BLASPHEMY of ATHEISTS

500 Greatest Quips and Quotes from Freethinkers, Non-Believers and the Happily Damned

Compiled by
Jonathan C. Criswell

Ulysses Press

Published in the United States by
ULYSSES PRESS
P.O. Box 3440
Berkeley, CA 94703
www.ulyssespress.com

ISBN: 978-1-56975-901-1
Library of Congress Catalog Number 2011921435

Acquisitions Editor: Kelly Reed
Managing Editor: Claire Chun
Editors: Sayre Van Young, Lauren Harrison
Design: what!design @ whatweb.com
Production: Judith Metzener
Cover photos: gold texture © naphtalina/istockphoto.com;
        crackled paint © Soubrette/istockphoto.com; icon of
        Jesus Christ © kadmy/istockphoto.com

Printed in Canada by Webcom

10 9 8 7 6 5 4 3 2 1

Distributed by Publishers Group West

This book is dedicated to all those who *know*
they *don't know*.

Introduction

I guess I've always been a collector. When I was a kid, it was baseball caps and cowboy hats. In my preteen years, I began reading, and reading a lot. I wasn't just satisfied with reading books. I had to own them, and thus, I began building a personal library at a young age. The more I read, the more my innocent and naïve mind grew. Soon I began to question everything. I questioned the things I read in books, the things told to me in classrooms, and finally, the things being preached to me from behind the Sunday pulpit. It just so happened that the preacher was my father.

My questions about God, Christianity, the Bible, and other religions were largely suppressed, but I wasn't satisfied. So I read everything I could on religion and soon discovered that there are (and have been) a lot of others just like me. They are called "freethinkers," "humanists," "atheists," "agnostics," and oh yeah, "sinners," according to my parents. I discovered that atheist thought extends back to the beginning of written history. Most importantly, I discovered that it is okay to question everything. Questioning is the catalyst of creativity, and all great discovery and original thought finds its origins in deliberate reflection. Finally, by the time I began university, I came out of the closet and proclaimed my skepticism. Nearly two decades later, I'm now comfortable with the lack of "God" in my life and in the world, and enjoy passively proselytizing atheist contemplation.

A few years ago, I was engaged in an e-mail battle with a religious friend about the goodness of God (or in my case, the inherent evil of the supposed being). In one of my retorts, I wrote, "Since 99.9% of cries to God are never answered, what appears to be answered prayer is nothing more than a statistical anomaly." My friend e-mailed back, "That was good...you should write it down."

So I did. After jotting down that first quote, I started collecting any passage, reading, or line that was remotely acrimonious, spiteful, and the antithesis of religious doctrine. After a few months, my list had grown to more than a hundred. I kept reading, researching, and compiling quotes, and the outcome is what you now have your hand, *The Wit and Blasphemy of Atheists*. The hundreds of quotes contained in this volume are biting and irreverent; some are funny and some might make you grimace; but they all share one thing in common: They are antidotes to religion and those who practice it.

This project turned out to be a lot of fun to put together. It reminded me of my youthful search for "true knowledge." It reminded me that there are so many others who enjoy fully functional lives without a deity governing their every whim. It reminded me that there is a several-thousand-year-old record of those who oppose believing what someone else says is true just because they say so. Please enjoy this collection as much as I've enjoyed compiling it. And remember, "True knowledge begins when the fear of God ends."

Jonathan C. Criswell
Greenville, South Carolina
January 2011

Remember my child, true knowledge begins when
the fear of God ends.
        —*Edward Babinski*

A celibate clergy is an especially good idea, because
it tends to suppress any hereditary propensity
towards fanaticism.
        —*Carl Sagan*

Aware of light and yet condemned to grope
Through dark regression's cave, told she must find
Life's purpose in that blackness, without hope,
Denied the luminescence of her mind
Until, at last, she finds the darkness kind,
Religion's child—a babe once bright and fair,
Curls up, tucks in her tail, and says her prayer.
        —*Sherry Matulis*

I was raised in the Jewish tradition, taught never to marry a Gentile woman, shave on Saturday, and most especially, never to shave a Gentile woman on Saturday.
—*Woody Allen*

If absolute power corrupts absolutely, where does that leave God?
—*George Deacon*

The ethical view of the universe involves us at last in so many cruel and absurd contradictions … that I have come to suspect that the aim of creation cannot be ethical at all.
—*Joseph Conrad*

I didn't think you existed.
>—*Julianne Moore, when asked what she*
>*would say to God at the Pearly Gates*

Prayers are to men as dolls are to children. They are not without use and comfort, but it is not easy to take them seriously.
>—*Samuel Butler*

Faith, *n*. Belief without evidence in what is told by one who speaks without knowledge, of things without parallel.
>—*Ambrose Bierce*

A jealous lover of human liberty, deeming it the absolute condition of all that we admire and respect in humanity, I reverse the phrase of Voltaire, and say that, if God really existed, it would be necessary to abolish him.
　　　—*Mikhail Bakunin*

Finding that no religion is based on facts and cannot be true, I began to reflect what must be the condition of mankind trained from infancy to believe in error.
　　　—*Robert Owen*

What can be taking place in the minds of such intelligent men that leads them to become so stupid!
　　　—*Camille Pissarro, when asked about what he thought about God*

That the not adhering to those notions reason
dictates concerning the nature of God, has been
the occasion of all superstition, and all those
innumerable mischiefs that mankind, on the
account of religion, have done either to themselves,
or one another.
—*Matthew Tindal*

The most tedious of all discourses are on the
subject of the Supreme Being.
—*Ralph Waldo Emerson*

Religion is a means of exploitation employed by
the strong against the weak; religion is a cloak of
ambition, injustice and vice…. Truth breaks free,
science is popularized, and religion totters; soon it
will fall…. In good time we shall only have to deal
with reason.
—*Georges Bizet*

Only Puritans think of the Devil as the most fascinating figure in the universe.
— *Heywood C. Broun*

Man has been forced to vegetate in his primitive stupidity; he has been taught stories about invisible powers upon whom his happiness was supposed to depend. Occupied solely by his fears, and by unintelligible reveries, he has always been at the mercy of priests, who have reserved to themselves the right of thinking for him, and of directing his actions.
— *Baron d'Holbach*

"Quotations taken from the Authorized Version (1611) of the Bible unless otherwise stated." What do you mean? There are unauthorized versions? And who's checking? God?
    —*Unknown*

Although the time of death is approaching me, I am not afraid of dying and going to Hell or (what would be considerably worse) going to the popularized version of Heaven. I expect death to be nothingness and, for removing me from all possible fears of death, I am thankful to atheism.
    —*Isaac Asimov*

If God wanted people to believe in him, why'd he invent logic then?
    —*David Feherty*

Christ, according to the faith, is the second person in the Trinity, the Father being the first and the Holy Ghost the third. Each of these three persons is God. Christ is his own father and his own son. The Holy Ghost is neither father nor son, but both. The son was begotten by the father, but existed before he was begotten—just the same before as after....

So, it is declared that the Father is God and the Son God, and the Holy Ghost God, and that these three Gods make one God.

According to the celestial multiplication table, once one is three, and three times one is one, and according to heavenly subtraction if we take two from three, three are left. The addition is equally peculiar, if we add two to one we have but one. Nothing ever was, nothing ever can be more perfectly idiotic and absurd than the dogma of the Trinity.

—*Robert Ingersoll*

The kind of fraud which consists in daring to proclaim the truth while mixing it with a large share of lies that falsify it, is more widespread than is generally thought.
—*Marcel Proust*

Infidel, *n*. In New York, one who does not believe in the Christian religion; in Constantinople, one who does.
—*Ambrose Bierce*

They that approve a private opinion, call it opinion; but they that mislike it, heresy: and yet heresy signifies no more than private opinion.
—*Thomas Hobbes*

One should not go to church if one wants to breathe *pure* air.
  —*Friedrich Nietzsche*

[As a young man] I came to the conclusion that the church was just a bunch of fascists ... I stopped going on Sunday mornings and watched the birds with my father instead.
  —*Dr. James Watson*

Here's what happens when you die—you sit in a box and get eaten by worms. I guarantee you that when you die, nothing cool happens.
  —*Howard Stern*

Televangelists: the pro wrestlers of religion.
—*Steven Wright*

I don't pray because I don't want to bore God.
—*Orson Welles*

I would love to believe that when I die I will live again, that some thinking, feeling, remembering part of me will continue. But as much as I want to believe that, and despite the ancient and worldwide cultural traditions that assert an afterlife, I know of nothing to suggest that it is more than wishful thinking.
—*Carl Sagan*

Whatever a man prays for, he prays for a miracle. Every prayer reduces itself to this: Great God, grant that twice two be not four.
—*Ivan Turgenev*

The creationists have this creator who is evil, who is small-minded, who is malevolent, and who is not very bright and can't even get his science right. Creationists have made their creator in their own image, in my view.
—*Ian Plimer*

I am convinced that the bright future of mankind is connected with the progress of science, and I believe it is inevitable that one day religions (at least those existing now) will drop in status to no higher than that of astrology.
—*Vitaly Lazarevich Ginzburg*

I contend that we are both atheists, I just believe in one fewer god than you do. When you understand why you dismiss all the other possible gods, you will understand why I dismiss yours.
　　—*Stephen F. Roberts*

All thinking men are atheists.
　　—*Ernest Hemingway*

Since 99.9% of cries to God are never answered, what appears to be answered prayer is nothing more than a statistical anomaly.
　　—*Jonathan C. Criswell*

Surely the ass who invented the first religion ought
to be the first ass damned.
   —*Mark Twain*

I dislike blasphemy on purely rational grounds.
If there is no God, blasphemy is stupid and
unnecessary; if there is, then it's damned
dangerous.
   —*Flann O'Brien*

Christianity, as many religions, was just
dreamed up by a couple people with really good
imaginations, a lot of time on their hands, and even
some "herbal" help. I mean, who would dream up
half of that crap without being totally baked?
   —*Jillian A. Spencer*

Organized religion is a sham and a crutch for weak-minded people who need strength in numbers. It tells people to go out and stick their noses in other people's business.
>—*Jesse Ventura*

Neither in my private life nor in my writings, have I ever made a secret of being an out-and-out unbeliever.
>—*Sigmund Freud*

If revealed religions have revealed anything it is that they are usually wrong.
>—*Francis Crick*

This young fellow, who is possessed of most violent passions, which he with great difficulty can command, and of unbounded ambition, which he conceals perhaps even to himself, has been seduced into that bigoted, illiberal system of religion, which, by professing vainly to follow purely the dictates of the Bible, in reality contradicts the whole doctrine of the New Testament, and destroys all the boundaries between good and evil, between right and wrong. But, like all the followers of that sect, his practice is at open variance with his theory. When I observe into what inconsistent absurdities those persons run who make speculative, metaphysical religion a matter of importance, I am fully determined never to puzzle myself in the mazes of religious discussion, to content myself with practicing the dictates of God and reason so far as I can judge for myself....

—*John Quincy Adams*

Which religion do I profess to follow? None! And
why? Because of religion.
—*Friedrich von Schiller*

The luckiest thing that ever happened to me
was that my father didn't believe in God, and
so he had no hang-ups about souls. I see
ourselves as products of evolution, which itself is
a great mystery.
—*Dr. James Watson*

… the mysteries, on belief in which theology would
hang the destinies of mankind, are cunningly
devised fables whose origin and growth are
traceable to the age of ignorance, the mother
of credulity.
—*Edward Clodd*

I reject Christianity's anthropomorphic God, made in our image, silly and malicious, vain and puerile, irritable or tender, after our fashion.
—*George Sand*

… the very fears and guilts imposed by religious training are responsible for some of history's most brutal wars, crusades, pogroms, and persecutions, including five centuries of almost unimaginable terrorism under Europe's Inquisition and the unthinkably sadistic legal murder of nearly nine million women. History doesn't say much very good about God.
—*Barbara G. Walker*

Gullibility and credulity are considered undesirable qualities in every department of human life— except religion. Why are we praised by godly men for surrendering our "godly gift" of reason when we cross their mental thresholds?
　　　—*Christopher Hitchens*

Free thought means fearless thought. It is not deterred by legal penalties, nor by spiritual consequences.
　　　—*George Jacob Holyoake*

Question with boldness even the existence of a god; because, if there be one, he must more approve of the homage of reason, than that of blindfolded fear.
　　　—*Thomas Jefferson*

When one guy sees an invisible man, he's a nut case. Ten people see him it's a cult. Ten million people see him it's a respected religion.
　　　　—*Richard Jeni*

What a tragedy it is to invent a God and then suffer to keep him King.
　　　　—*Rod Steiger*

I don't believe in god. I don't believe in an afterlife. I don't believe in soul. I don't believe in anything. I think it's totally right for people to have their own beliefs if it makes them happy, but to me it's a pretty preposterous idea.
　　　　—*Joaquin Phoenix*

My own view on religion is that of Lucretius. I regard it as a disease born of fear and as a source of untold misery to the human race.
—*Bertrand Russell*

Although we weren't brought up to be any particular religion, we were taught to say our prayers. I remember one that ended, "Thy glorious kingdom, which is forever and ever. Amen."
These words made me scream, "I don't want to be anywhere forever and ever." It's too much.
—*Hermione Gingold*

"Faith" is a fine invention
When Gentlemen can *see*—
But *Microscopes* are prudent
In an Emergency.
—*Emily Dickinson*

The human mind is greater than any book. The mind sits in judgment on every book. If there be truth in the book, we take it; if error, we discard it. Why refer this to the Bible? In this country, the Bible has been used to support slavery and capital punishment; while in the old countries, it has been quoted to sustain all manner of tyranny and persecution. All reforms are anti-Bible. We must look at all things rationally.
　　　—*William Lloyd Garrison*

The belief that there is only one truth and that oneself is in possession of it, seems to me the deepest root of all evil in the world.
　　　—*Max Born*

… I can't admit of an old boy of a God who takes walks in his garden with a cane in his hand, who lodges his friends in the belly of whales, dies uttering a cry, and rises again after three days; things absurd in themselves, and completely opposed, moreover, to all physical laws, which proves to us, by the way, that priests have always wallowed in squalid ignorance, and tried to drag whole civilizations down after them.

—*Gustave Flaubert*

The greatest contribution nonbelievers have made to the world has been the Constitution of the United States. Consider how very heretical to a religious world was the idea of a Constitution predicated on "We, the People."

—*Queen Silver*

And God said, "Let there be light" and there was light, but the Electricity Board said He would have to wait until Thursday to be connected.
—*Spike Milligan*

To you I'm an atheist … ; to God I'm the loyal opposition.
—*Woody Allen*

… the religion of one age is, as a rule, the literary entertainment of the next….
—*Fridtjof Nansen*

God is love, but get it in writing.
—*Gypsy Rose Lee*

… heaven for climate, and hell for society.
　　　—Mark Twain

If God really wanted us to watch those Sunday
morning religious shows, he'd make the reception
better than the cartoons on the other channels.
　　　—Michael E. Nelson

Sometimes I lie awake at night and ask, "Where
have I gone wrong?" Then a voice says to me, "This
is going to take more than one night."
　　　—Charlie Brown, in the Peanuts *comic strip*

The WIT and BLASPHEMY of ATHEISTS

There in Rangoon I realized that the gods
were enemies, just like God,
of the poor human being.
Gods
in alabaster extended
like white whales,
gods gilded like spikes,
serpent gods entwining
the crime of being born,
naked and elegant buddhas
smiling at the cocktail party
of empty eternity
like Christ on his horrible cross,
all of them capable of anything,
of imposing on us their heaven,
all with torture or pistol
to purchase piety or burn our blood,
fierce gods made by men
to conceal their cowardice,
and there it was all like that,
the whole earth reeking of heaven,
and heavenly merchandise.
　　　　　—*Pablo Neruda*

How do you play religious roulette? You stand around in a circle and blaspheme and see who gets struck by lightning first.
> —*Unknown*

Missionaries are perfect nuisances and leave every place worse than they found it.
> —*Charles Dickens*

I have seldom met an intelligent person whose views were not narrowed and distorted by religion.
> —*James Buchanan*

I took a sheet of paper, divided it into debt and credit columns on the arguments for and against God and immortality…. I wrote "bankrupt" at the foot … from that hour on I have been wholly free from the nightmare of doubt that had lain on me for years.

—*Joseph McCabe*

I admire anyone who's genuinely trying to achieve spiritual enlightenment and live a peaceful life. But religious dogma is a barrier to that. The last thing a dogmatist wants is for anyone to be enlightened, any more than a pharmaceutical company wants anybody cured.

—*Pat Condell*

It took me years, but letting go of religion has been the most profound wake up of my life. I feel I now look at the world not as a child, but as an adult. I see what's bad and it's really bad. But I also see what is beautiful, what is wonderful. And I feel so deeply appreciative that I am alive. How dare the religious use the term "born again." That truly describes freethinkers who've thrown off the shackles of religion so much better!

—*Julia Sweeney*

Is man one of God's blunders? Or is God one of man's blunders?

—*Friedrich Nietzsche*

All religions promise a reward beyond this life
in eternity for excellences of the *will* or of the
heart, but none for excellences of the head, of the
understanding.
　　　—*Arthur Schopenhauer*

Religion is the idol of the mob; it adores everything
it does not understand.... We know the crimes that
fanaticism in religion has caused ...
　　　—*Frederick the Great*

The merits and services of Christianity have been
industriously extolled by its hired advocates ...
it has induced a general tendency to allow its
pretensions without inquiry and its beneficence
without proof.
　　　—*J. M. Wheeler*

I read the book of Job last night—I don't think God comes well out of it.
   —*Virginia Woolf*

Emancipate thy mind from the idle fears of superstition, and the wicked arts of Priesthood.
   —*John Baskerville*

The sooner you get rid of all this Christian humbug the better. The whole traditional conception of life is false. Throw those great Christian blinkers away, and look around you and stand on your own feet and be a man…. Don't believe all the tommyrot preachers tell you; learn and prove everything by your own experience…. One thing is certain—that English music will never be any good till they get rid of Jesus. Humanity is incredible. It will believe anything, anything to escape reality.
   —*Frederick Delius*

"The Good Book"—one of the most remarkable euphemisms ever coined.
—*Ashley Montagu*

Anyone who knows history … will, I think, recognize that the domination of education or of government by any one particular religious faith is never a happy arrangement for the people.
—*Eleanor Roosevelt*

None of the beliefs in gods has any merit.
—*Paul D. Boyer*

If fifty million people say a foolish thing, it's still a foolish thing.
>   —*Anatole France (also attributed to Bertrand Russell)*

Be sweet to your mother at Xmas despite her early Chaldean rune-worship which she will undoubtedly inflict on you ...
>   —*F. Scott Fitzgerald*

Dissent from the Bible does not alarm the true investigator, who takes truth for authority not authority for truth.
>   —*George Jacob Holyoake*

I am an atheist, that is, I think nothing exists
except and beyond nature. Within the limits of my,
undoubtedly insufficient, knowledge of the history
of philosophy, I do not see, in fact, any difference
between atheism and the pantheism of Spinoza.
   —*Vitaly Lazarevich Ginzburg*

The thoughts of the gods are not more
unchangeable than those of the men who interpret
them. They advance—but they always lag behind
the thoughts of men.
   —*Anatole France*

Good God, how much reverence can you have for
a Supreme Being who finds it necessary to include
such phenomena as phlegm and tooth decay in His
divine system of creation?
   —*Joseph Heller*

Atheism strikes me as morally superior, as well as intellectually superior, to religion. Since it is obviously inconceivable that all religions can be right, the most reasonable conclusion is that they are all wrong.

    —*Christopher Hitchens*

There is not enough love and goodness in the world to permit us to give up any of that to idolatrous figments of our imagination.

    —*Friedrich Nietzsche*

You couldn't go out to play hopscotch or kick-the-can without tripping over a church or two. (Or a tavern. The churches had a reciprocal arrangement, I think....)

    —*Sherry Matulis, talking about her hometown of Nevada, Iowa*

Organized religions and their dogmas only serve to indoctrinate the participants into sheeplike common behaviors. This type of blind assimilation promotes the popularity of top-forty radio stations and movie sequels. Train your light spirit to shun God. Skepticism towards groups, holy or otherwise, is enriching and makes you a far more entertaining drinking companion.

—*Janeane Garofalo*

I am an atheist. I suppose you can call me a sort of libertarian anarchist. I regard religion with fear and suspicion. It's not enough to say I don't believe in god.... I am offended by some of the things said in the Bible and the Koran, and I refute them.

—*Emma Thompson*

This [Robert Ingersoll's *Essays and Lectures*] was an exciting discovery; his atheism confirmed my own belief that the horrific cruelty of the Old Testament was degrading to the human spirit.
—*Charlie Chaplin*

To hate man and worship God seems to be the sum of all the creeds.
—*Robert Ingersoll*

Faith may be defined briefly as an illogical belief in the occurrence of the improbable.
—*H. L. Mencken*

Talking to god is crazy.
Hearing god is schizophrenia.
Acting on it is insanity.
        —*Robert Patterson*

That's all religion is—some principle you believe in
… man has accomplished far more miracles than
the God he invented.
        —*Rod Steiger*

Please, with the God talk. Hate to break it to you,
but there is no God.
        —*Howard Stern*

Whether Socrates got as much out of life as
Wesley [John Wesley, founder of Methodism] is an
unanswerable question, but a nation of Socrateses
would be much safer and happier than a nation
of Wesleys.
        —*George Bernard Shaw*

Your church is a baby-house made of blocks ....
        —*Henry David Thoreau*

Christians are masters of *selective observation*—or
"counting the hits and ignoring the misses."
        —*David Mills*

Religion is the most malevolent of all mind viruses.
  —*Arthur C. Clarke*

No religion has ever given a picture of deity which men could have imitated without the grossest immorality.
  —*George Santayana*

Start out understanding religion by saying everything is possibly wrong…. As soon as you do that, you start sliding down an edge which is hard to recover from …
  —*Richard Feynman*

I'm an atheist, and that's *it*. I believe there's nothing we can know except that we should be kind to each other and do what we can for other people.
—*Katharine Hepburn*

The Church is now more like the Scribes and Pharisees than like Christ. What are now called "essential doctrines" of the Christian religion He does not even mention.
—*Florence Nightingale*

Evangelist, *n.* A bearer of good tidings, particularly (in a religious sense) such as assure us of our own salvation and the damnation of our neighbors.
—*Ambrose Bierce*

We would be 1,500 years ahead if it hadn't been for the church dragging science back by its coattails and burning our best minds at the stake.
—*Catherine Fahringer*

I would put faith in the same category [as alchemy] because faith is believing something without a good reason to believe it.
—*Steven Pinker*

I wondered a little why God was such a useless thing. It seemed a waste of time to have him. After that he became less and less, until he was … nothingness.
—*Frances Farmer*

There are a score of great religions in the world …
and each is a mighty fortress of graft.
>   —*Upton Sinclair*

When I was eight years old, I tried prayer. And it
didn't work!
>   —*Frances Hamerstrom*

I have four children, which is not bad considering
I'm not a Catholic.
>   —*Peter Ustinov*

The Methodist Discipline provides for "separate Colored Conferences." The Episcopal church shuts out some of its own most worthy ministers from clerical recognition, on account of their color. Nearly all denominations of religionists have either a written or unwritten law to the same effect. In Boston, even, there are Evangelical churches whose pews are positively forbidden by corporate mandate from being sold to any but "respectable white persons." Our incorporated cemeteries are often, if not always, deeded in the same manner. Even our humblest village grave yards generally have either a "negro corner," or refuse colored corpses altogether; and did our power extend to heaven or hell, we should have complexional salvation and colored damnation ....

  —*Parker Pillsbury*

I never yet have seen the person who could withstand the doubt and unbelief that enter his mind when reading the Bible in a spirit of inquiry.
   —*Etta Semple*

I'm an atheist…. How unfortunate it is to assign responsibility to the higher up for justice amongst people.
   —*Ani DiFranco*

I do not believe in God, because I believe in man. Whatever his mistakes, man has for thousands of years past been working to undo the botched job your god has made.
   —*Emma Goldman*

But as a torch-bearer, as a bringer of joy,
[Christianity] has been a failure. It has given
infinite consequences to the acts of finite beings,
crushing the soul with a responsibility too great for
mortals to bear. It has filled the future with fear
and flame, and made God the keeper of an eternal
penitentiary, destined to be the home of nearly
all the sons of man. Not satisfied with that, it has
deprived God of the pardoning power.
  —*Robert Ingersoll*

I maintain that thoughtful Atheism affords greater
possibility for human happiness than any system
yet based on, or possible to be founded on, Theism,
and that the lives of true Atheists must be more
virtuous—because more human—than those of the
believers in Deity....
  —*Charles Bradlaugh*

I am a Humanist and a freethinker because, as Mr.
Spock would say, it is only logical.
 —*Susan Sackett*

We have fought long and hard to escape from
medieval superstition. I, for one, do not wish to
go back.
 —*James Randi*

The Bible illustrated by Dore occupied many of
my hours—and I think probably gave me many
nightmares.
 —*Eleanor Roosevelt*

The only excuse for God is that he doesn't exist.
>   —*Friedrich Nietzsche (also attributed to Stendhal)*

A nation which thinks that it is belief in God and not good law which makes people honest does not seem to me very advanced.
>   —*Denis Diderot*

If triangles made a god, they would give him three sides.
>   —*Charles de Montesquieu*

I have struggled all my life with a tormented and joyless relationship with God. Faith and lack of faith, punishment, grace, and rejection, all were real to me, all were imperative. My prayers stank of anguish, entreaty, trust, loathing, and despair. God spoke, God said nothing…. No one is safe from religious ideas and confessional phenomena…. We can fall victim to them when we least expect it. It's like Mao's flu, or being struck by lightning…. You were born without purpose, you live without meaning, living is its own meaning. When you die, you are extinguished. From being you will be transformed to non-being. A god does not necessarily dwell among our capricious atoms.

—*Ingmar Bergman*

The Old Testament is responsible for more
atheism, agnosticism, disbelief—call it what you
will—than any book ever written; it has emptied
more churches than all the counterattractions of
cinema, motor bicycle and golf course.
—*A. A. Milne*

Let us begin, then, at once, with that merest of
words, "infinity." This, like "God," "spirit," and some
other expressions of which the equivalents exist
in all languages, is by no means the expression of
an idea, but of an effort at one. It stands for the
possible attempt at an impossible conception.
—*Edgar Allen Poe*

When I hear … from people that it [religion] doesn't hurt anything, I say, "Really?" Well, besides wars, the Crusades, the Inquisitions, 9-11, ethnic cleansing, the suppression of women, the suppression of homosexuals, fatwas, honor killings, suicide bombings, arranged marriages to minors, human sacrifice, burning witches, and systematic sex with children, I have a few little quibbles. And I forgot blowing up girls schools in Afghanistan.
—*Bill Maher*

If you talk to God, you are praying; if God talks to you, you have schizophrenia.
—*Thomas Szasz*

History has the relation to truth that theology has to religion—i.e., none to speak of.
—*Robert A. Heinlein*

In the Bible, the ones who were most certain about what they were doing were the ones who stoned the prophets.
>—*Bob Chell*

The Jews are nervous people. Nineteen centuries of Christian love have taken a toll.
>—*Benjamin Disraeli*

My son, always respect and honor the other fellow's point of view. Unless it's different from yours, of course.
>—*Hagar, in the* Hagar the Horrible
> *comic strip*

Truth, not tolerance.
> —*Bumper sticker that shows a clenched fist on the left side and a Christian cross on the right.*

Of all *isms* I think dogmatism the worst.
> —*George Jacob Holyoake*

Christianity did not come with tidings of great joy, but with a message of eternal grief. It came with the threat of everlasting torture on its lips. It meant war on earth and perdition hereafter.
> —*Robert Ingersoll*

When a mere girl, my mother offered me a dollar
if I would read the Bible through;…despairing
of reconciling many of its absurd statements
with even my childish philosophy;…I gave the
dollar back, and became a skeptic, doubter, and
unbeliever long ere the "Good Book" was ended.
—*Elmina D. Slenker*

The personages of the Christian Heaven and their
conversations are no more matter of fact than
the personages of the Greek Olympus and their
conversations.
—*Matthew Arnold*

Sure. I think it's like a movie that was way too popular. It's a story that's been told too many times and just doesn't mean anything. Man lived on the planet—[*placing his fingers an inch apart*], this is 5,000 years of semirecorded history. And God and the Bible, that came in somewhere around the middle, maybe 2,000. This is the last 2,000, this is what we're about to celebrate [*indicating about an eighth of an inch with his fingers*]. Now, humans, in some shape or form, have been on the earth for three million years [*pointing across the room to indicate the distance*]. So, all this time, from there [*gesturing toward the other side of the room*], to here [*indicating the eighth of an inch*], there was no God, there was no story, there was no myth and people lived on this planet and they wandered and they gathered and they did all these things. The planet was never threatened. How did they survive for all this time without this belief in God? That just seems funny to me.

> —*Eddie Vedder, when asked what he thought about God*

Where it is a duty to worship the sun, it is pretty
sure to be a crime to examine the laws of heat.
  —*John Morley*

It was only when I finally undertook to read
the Bible through from beginning to end that I
perceived that its depiction of the Lord God—
whom I had always viewed as the very embodiment
of perfection—was actually that of a monstrous,
vengeful tyrant, far exceeding in bloodthirstiness
and insane savagery the depredations of Hitler,
Stalin, Pol Pot, Attila the Hun, or any other mass
murderer of ancient or modern history.
  —*Steve Allen*

I lost my faith during the war, and can't believe
they are all up there, flying around or sitting at
tables, all those I've lost.
—*Marlene Dietrich*

The earth is flat, and anyone who disputes this
claim is an atheist who deserves to be punished.
—*Sheikh Abdel-Aziz Ibn Baaz*

As the post said, "Only God can make a tree,"
probably because it's so hard to figure out how to
get the bark on.
—*Woody Allen*

When we hear the ancient bells growling on a
Sunday morning we ask ourselves: Is it really
possible! This, for a Jew, crucified two thousand
years ago, who said he was God's son? The proof
of such a claim is lacking. Certainly the Christian
religion is an antiquity projected into our times
from remote prehistory; and the fact that the claim
is believed—whereas one is otherwise so strict
in examining pretensions—is perhaps the most
ancient piece of this heritage. A god who begets
children with a mortal woman; a sage who bids
men work no more, have no more courts, but look
for the signs of the impending end of the world;
a justice that accepts the innocent as a vicarious
sacrifice; someone who orders his disciples to drink
his blood; prayers for miraculous interventions; sins
perpetrated against a god, atoned for by a god; fear
of a beyond to which death is the portal; the form
of the cross as a symbol in a time that no longer
knows the function and ignominy of the cross—
how ghoulishly all this touches us, as if from the
tomb of a primeval past! Can one believe that such
things are still believed?
—*Friedrich Nietzsche*

When the missionaries came to Africa they had the Bible and we had the land. They said, "Let us pray." We closed our eyes. When we opened them, we had the Bible and they had the land.

— *Bishop Desmond Tutu*

Family, friends, and well-wishers from around the world assured me that prayers and my faith in God would comfort me. I tried to pray but I didn't feel any better, nor did I make any kind of connection with God.

—*Christopher Reeve*

Religion and government will both exist in greater purity, the less they are mixed together.

—*James Madison*

I'm Jewish. I don't work out. If God had wanted us to bend over, He would of put diamonds on the floor.

—*Joan Rivers*

Not only have the "followers" of Christ made it their rule to hack to bits all those who do not accept their beliefs, they have also ferociously massacred each other, in the name of their common "religion of love," under banners proclaiming their faith in Him who had expressly commanded them to love one another.

—*Georges Clemenceau*

Religious belief is a fine guide around which a person might organize his or her own life, but an awful instrument around which to organize someone else's life.

—*Richard D. Mohr*

The idea that a country or a people could somehow be ordained by heaven to commit unspeakable acts in God's name is insane. Unfortunately, history is full of inhuman acts by religious leaders in the name of their dogma or holy war. Only when the world accepts there are no chosen people and no chosen religions will we earn the right to call ourselves human beings.

 —*Zain Winter*

Support your local pedophile—attend a Catholic Church.

 —*Bumper sticker*

So far as I can remember, there is not one word in the Gospels in praise of intelligence.

 —*Bertrand Russell*

God is a comedian playing to an audience that's too afraid to laugh.
>   —*Voltaire*

The secret of a good sermon is to have a good beginning and a good ending, then having the two as close together as possible.
>   —*George Burns*

Oh Lord, deliver me from thy followers.
>   —*Bumper sticker*

Religions are like glow worms: they shine only when it's dark.
>   —*Arthur Schopenhauer*

Women have never invented a religion; they are
untainted with that madness....
—*George Augustus Moore*

Man is certainly stark mad. He cannot make a flea,
and yet he will be making gods by the dozen.
—*Michel de Montaigne*

The louder he talked of his honor, the faster we
counted our spoons.
—*Ralph Waldo Emerson*

Oh, threats of hell and hopes of paradise!
One thing at least is certain—this life flies;
One thing is certain, and the rest is lies.
—*Omar Khayyam*

I believe that when I die I shall rot, and nothing of my ego will survive.
　　　　—*Bertrand Russell*

Reverence, *n*. The spiritual attitude of a man to a god and a dog to a man.
　　　　—*Ambrose Bierce*

… a large portion of the noblest and most valuable teaching has been the work, not only of men who did not know, but of men who knew and rejected, the Christian faith.
　　　　—*John Stuart Mill*

[At parochial school] I was told I had an
overabundance of original sin.
   —*Susan Sarandon*

I find that life is rich, diverse, fabulous, and
extraordinary, conceived without a god.
   —*Ian McEwan*

Freedom of religion includes freedom from
religion.... Why don't we celebrate living, instead of
worrying about damnation and sin?
   —*Ed Schempp*

You find as you look around the world that every
single bit of progress of humane feeling, every
improvement in the criminal law, every step toward
the diminution of war, every step toward better
treatment of the colored races, or every mitigation
of slavery, every moral progress that there has been
in the world, has been consistently opposed by
the organized churches of the world. I say quite
deliberately that the Christian religion, as organized
in its churches, has been and still is the principal
enemy of moral progress in the world.

—*Bertrand Russell*

As long as the priest is considered a *higher* type
of man—this *professional* negator, slanderer,
and poisoner of life—there is no answer to the
question: What is Truth?

—*Friedrich Nietzsche*

I'm sure there are all sorts of higher powers like electromagnetism and gravity, and things like that. But I don't believe in a deity, no. I see no evidence for that in my life or anywhere else in the universe.... I find that most deism, and certainly most theisms take a fairly narrow view of the universe, and most people's views of God or gods seem to be rather impoverished. The universe itself, the physical world that we can perceive with our senses and grasp with our minds, seems to be far more wondrous then most people's conceptions of a deity.

—*Ronald Reagan, Jr.*

Know then thyself, presume not God to scan,
The proper study of mankind is Man.

—*Alexander Pope*

You never see animals going through the absurd
and often horrible fooleries of magic and religion
… Asses do not bray a liturgy to cloudless skies.
Nor do cats attempt, by abstinence from cat's meat,
to wheedle the feline spirits into benevolence. Only
man behaves with such gratuitous folly. It is the
price he has to pay for being intelligent but not, as
yet, quite intelligent enough.
  —*Aldous Huxley*

Nowadays, you can say practically anything about
Jesus without creating offense—so long as you
admit he existed. There was no such person.
  —*G. A. Wells*

Give me truth; cheat me by no illusion.
  —*Margaret Fuller*

The dull pray; the geniuses are light mockers.
       —*Ralph Waldo Emerson*

If some good evidence for life after death were
announced, I'd be eager to examine it; but it would
have to be real scientific data, not mere anecdote.
As with the face on Mars and alien abductions,
better the hard truth, I say, than the comforting
fantasy. And in the final tolling it often turns out
that the facts are more comforting than the fantasy.
       —*Carl Sagan*

[The Bible] is full of interest. It has noble poetry
in it; and some clever fables; and some
blood-drenched history; and some good morals;
and a wealth of obscenity; and upwards of a
thousand lies.
       —*Mark Twain*

We recognise no authority competent to dictate to us. Each must believe what he considers to be true and act up to his belief, granting the same right to everyone else.

—*Robert Stout*

Never was the day, never, in all the tide of time, in which such mighty efforts were made to keep mankind in ignorance; never were any clergy on earth, Pagan or Papistical, so opposed to the diffusion of knowledge, so desperately afraid of it, and so bitterly hostile to it, as the Protestant clergy, both of the established church, and the dissenters of the present day....

—*Robert Taylor*

The beauty of religious mania is that it has the power to explain everything. Once God (or Satan) is accepted as the first cause of everything which happens in the mortal world, nothing is left to chance...logic can be happily tossed out the window.
　　　　　—Stephen King

If there is no God, who pops up the next Kleenex?
　　　　　—Art Hoppe

I still say a church steeple with a lightening rod on top shows a lack of confidence.
　　　　　—Doug McLeod

Probably no invention came more easily to man than Heaven.
—*Unknown*

Atheism, properly understood, is in nowise a cold, barren negative; it is, on the contrary, a hearty, fruitful affirmation of all truth, and involves the positive assertion and action of highest humanity.
—*Charles Bradlaugh*

If anyone … believes that God made his body, and your body is dirty, the fault lies with the manufacturer.
—*Lenny Bruce*

Most of us spend the first six days of the week sowing wild oats, and then we go to church on Sunday and pray for crop failure.
—*Fred Allen*

The whole idea of god is absurd. What some people call "god" is simply an acceptable term for their ignorance. What they don't understand, they call "god."
—*Stanley Kubrick*

I have managed most of my life to exclude religious speculation from my mode of thought. I've found that, on the whole, it adds very little to economics.
—*John Kenneth Galbraith*

Religions are matters for the mob; after coming in contact with a religious man, I always feel that I must wash my hands.
— *Friedrich Nietzsche*

Eskimo: If I did not know about God and sin, would I go to hell?
Priest: No, not if you didn't know.
Eskimo: Then why did you tell me?
— *Annie Dillard*

I've been so relieved and so grateful to not have a god to believe in.
— *Cloris Leachman*

The Christian religion not only was at first attended with miracles, but even at this day cannot be believed by any reasonable person without one.
   —*David Hume*

Religion has kept civilization back for thousands of years, and the biggest mistake in the history of civilization is ethical monotheism, the concept of the one God. Let's get rid of it and be rational.
   —*Peter Watson*

Do you have any weapons, flammable materials or hazardous religious beliefs?
   —*Don Addis cartoon showing an American Indian checking a* Mayflower *Pilgrim's trunk*

… I regard monotheism as the greatest disaster
ever to befall the human race.
   —*Gore Vidal*

Religion disapproves of original thought the way
Dracula disapproves of sunlight.
   —*Pat Condell*

So urgent … is the necessity of believing, that the
fall of any system of mythology will most probably
be succeeded by the introduction of some other
mode of superstition.
   —*Edward Gibbon*

Any fool can make a rule, and any fool will mind it.
—*Henry David Thoreau*

There is charm about the forbidden that makes it unspeakably desirable.
—*Mark Twain*

… no kingdom has ever had as many civil wars as the kingdom of Christ.
—*Charles de Montesquieu*

Science is the record of dead religions.
—*Oscar Wilde*

As for those who protest that I am robbing people of the great comfort and consolation they gain from Christianity, I can only say that Christianity includes hell, eternal torture for the vast majority of humanity, for most of your relatives and friends. Christianity includes a devil who is really more powerful than God, and who keeps gathering into his furnaces most of the creatures whom God turns out and for whom he sent his son to the cross in vain. If I could feel that I had robbed anybody of his faith in hell, I should not be ashamed or regretful.

—*Rupert Hughes*

With the religious you can hardly negotiate. They think they have supreme permission to kill people and go to war.

—*Shimon Peres*

With soap, baptism is a good thing.
  —*Robert Ingersoll*

When I started understanding how science works,
it occurred to me that there just is no evidence that
there is a God.
  —*Ben Bova*

Prayers never bring anything…. They may bring
solace to the sap, the bigot, the ignorant, the
aboriginal, and the lazy—but to the enlightened
it is the same as asking Santa Claus to bring you
something for Xmas.
  —*W. C. Fields*

Whenever we read the obscene stories, the voluptuous debaucheries, the cruel and torturous executions, the unrelenting vindictiveness, with which more than half the Bible is filled, it would be more consistent that we called it the word of a Demon than the word of God.
> —*Thomas Paine*

I was a woman, a divorcee, a socialist, an agnostic… all possible sins together.
> —*Michelle Bachelet*

Formidable as the task may seem at present, the long-term need is to persuade Americans that having evidence for your beliefs is a good idea.
> —*Peter Singer*

Jonathan C. Criswell

Listen, Christ,
You did alright in your day, I reckon—
But that day's gone now.
They ghosted you up a swell story, too,
Called it Bible—
But it's dead now.
The popes and the preachers've
Made too much money from it.
They've sold you to too many....
       —Langston Hughes

I know that a creed is the shell of a lie.
       —Amy Lowell

A cult is a religion with no political power.
       —Tom Wolfe

I was thinking about how people seem to read the
Bible a whole lot more as they get older; then it
dawned on me ... they're cramming for their
final exam.
—*George Carlin*

All gods from time immemorial are fantasies,
created by humans for the welfare of humans and
to attempt to explain the seemingly inexplicable.
But do we, ... in the 21st century of the Common
Era and on the springboard of colonising the
universe, need such palliatives?
—*Ludovic Kennedy*

I would of made a good pope.
—*Richard Nixon*

When did I realize I was God? Well, I was praying and I suddenly realized I was talking to myself.
  —*Peter O'Toole*

Puritanism, *n.* The haunting fear that someone, somewhere may be happy.
  —*Ambrose Bierce*

Some people are kind, polite, and sweet-spirited ... until you try to get into their pew.
  —*George Goldtrap*

My dear child, you must believe in God in spite of what the clergy tell you.
　　—*Benjamin Jowett*

When the Devil quotes Scriptures, it's not, really, to deceive, but simply that the masses are so ignorant of theology that somebody has to teach them the elementary texts before he can seduce them.
　　—*Paul Goodman*

Truth, in matters of religion, is simply the opinion that has survived.
　　—*Oscar Wilde*

The clergy, no less than the capitalist class, lives on the backs of the people, profits from the degradation, the ignorance and the oppression of the people.
>   —*Rosa Luxemburg*

A certain degree of general ignorance is the condition for the existence of any religion, the element in which alone it is able to exist.
>   —*Arthur Schopenhauer*

All intelligent hell would be better than a stupid paradise.
>   —*Victor Hugo*

But as a scientist, I can not help feeling that all religions are on a tottering foundation. None is perfect or inspired.
    —*Luther Burbank*

And "god-seeking" should be for the time being put aside—it is a useless occupation: it's no use seeking where there is nothing to be found.
    —*Maxim Gorky*

There ain't no devil, it's just god when he's drunk.
    —*Bumper sticker*

A religious person is a dangerous person. He may not become a thief or a murderer, but he is liable to become a nuisance. He carries with him many foolish and harmful superstitions, and he is possessed with the notion that it is his duty to give these superstitions to others.
—*Marilla M. Ricker*

Organized religions … are dying forms. They were all very important when we didn't know why the sun moved, why weather changed, why hurricanes occurred, or volcanoes happened. Modern religion is the end trail of modern mythology.
—*Bruce Willis*

If faith can not be reconciled with rational thinking, it has to be eliminated as an anachronistic remnant of earlier stages of culture and replaced by science dealing with facts and theories which are intelligible and can be validated.
—*Erich Fromm*

We never do evil so completely and cheerfully as when we do it out of conscience.
—*Blaise Pascal*

It's an incredible con job, when you think of it, to believe something now in exchange for life after death. Even corporations, with all their reward systems, don't try to make it posthumous.
—*Gloria Steinem*

To judge from the notions expounded by theologians, one must conclude that God created most men simply with a view to crowding hell.
—*Marquis de Sade*

If I were hungry and friendless today, I would rather take my chances with a saloon-keeper than with the average preacher.
-*Eugene V. Debs*

As the French say, there are three sexes: men, women, and clergymen.
—*Sydney Smith*

Most Texans think Hanukkah is some sort of
duck call.
—*Richard Lewis*

One thing I have no worry about is whether God
exists. But is has occurred to me that God has
Alzheimer's and has forgotten we exist.
—*Jane Wagner*

I once wanted to become an atheist but I gave up
... they have no holidays.
—*Henny Youngman*

I don't believe in God because I don't believe in Mother Goose.
  —*Clarence Darrow*

Christianity is such a silly religion.
  —*Gore Vidal*

The religious persecution of the ages has been carried on under what was claimed to be the command of God. I distrust those people who know so well what God wants them to do because it always coincides with their own desires.
  —*Susan B. Anthony*

The Church says the Earth is flat, but I know
that it is round, for I have seen the shadow of the
moon, and I have more faith in a shadow than in
the Church.
  —*Ferdinand Magellan*

Creeds are not guide-boards; they are tombstones.
On every creed can be read three words: "Here
lies"—and such lies!
  —*Marilla M. Ricker*

I think that piety is oppressive. It takes all the air
out of thought.
  —*Norman Mailer*

For more than three thousand years men have quarreled concerning the formulas of their faith. The earth has been drenched with blood shed in this cause, the face of day darkened with the blackness of the crimes perpetrated in its name. There have been no dirtier wars than religious wars, no bitterer hates than religious hates, no fiendish cruelty like religious cruelty; no baser baseness than religious baseness. It has destroyed the peace of families, turned the father against the son, the brother against the brother. And for what? Are we any nearer to unanimity? On the contrary, diversity within the churches and without has never been so widespread as at present. Sects and factions are multiplying on every hand, and every new schism is but the parent of a dozen others.

—*Felix Adler*

I got no religion in me. I could never see through it. Basically, I'm a facts man; if I can't see through it, I say it's not possible.

  —*J. R. Simplot*

To work hard, to live hard, to die hard, and then to go to hell after all would be too damned hard.

  —*Carl Sandburg*

Prayer seems to me a cry of weakness, and an attempt to avoid, by trickery, the rules of the game as laid down.

  —*Zora Neale Hurston*

Extraordinary claims require extraordinary evidence.
> —*Carl Sagan*

What is faith but believing in something without any evidence?
> —*Peter Singer*

… you adduce morality as a proof of God, and then cite God in support of morality. You reason in a beautiful circle, like a dog biting his own tail.
> —*Georg Buchner*

How can any woman believe that a loving and merciful God would, in one breath, command Eve to multiply and replenish the earth, and in the next, pronounce a curse upon her maternity?
　　—*Elizabeth Cady Stanton*

My views have changed from a belief that my prayers were heard, to clear atheism.... Over and over, expanding scientific knowledge has shown religious claims to be false.
　　—*Paul D. Boyer*

What I got in Sunday school … was simply a
firm conviction that the Christian faith was full
of palpable absurdities, and the Christian God
preposterous…. The act of worship, as carried on
by Christians, seems to me to be debasing rather
than ennobling. It involves groveling before a being
who, if he really exists, deserves to be denounced
instead of respected.
   —*H. L. Mencken*

Religion is a cradle of despotism.
   —*Marquis de Sade*

Everything's too damn expensive nowadays. Look
at this Bible I bought—fifteen bucks! And talk
about a preachy book! Everybody's a sinner, except
this guy.
   —*Homer, on* The Simpsons

Scratch the Christian and you'll find the pagan—spoiled.
                —*Israel Zangwill*

If it weren't for Christians, I'd be a Christian.
                —*Mahatma Gandi*

Had there been a lunatic asylum in the suburbs of Jerusalem, Jesus Christ would infallibly have been shut up in it at the outset of his public career. That interview with Satan on a pinnacle of the Temple would alone have damned him, and everything that happened after could but have confirmed the diagnosis. The whole religious complexion of the modern world is due to the absence from Jerusalem of a lunatic asylum.
                —*Havelock Ellis*

Goodbye,
Christ Jesus Lord God Jehovah,
Beat it on away from here now.
Make way for a new guy with no religion at all—
A real guy named
Marx Communist Lenin Peasant Stalin
    worker ME …
        —*Langston Hughes*

Science without religion is lame; religion without
science is blind.
        —*Albert Einstein*

To become a popular religion, it is only necessary
for a superstition to enslave a philosophy.
        —*William Ralph Inge*

Sweep aside those hatred-eaten mystics, who pose as friends of humanity and preach that the highest virtue man can practice is to hold his own life as of no value.
　　　—*Ayn Rand*

There ain't no answer. There ain't going to be any answer. There never has been an answer. That's the answer.
　　　—*Gertrude Stein, when asked about God*

It is impossible to exaggerate the evil work that theology has done in the world.
　　　—*Lydia Maria Child*

But it does not follow that the theology of a few should be allowed to forestall the health and well-being of the many.

—*Ronald Reagan, Jr.*

I cannot believe in the immortality of the soul.... I am an aggregate of cells, as for instance, New York City is an aggregate of individuals. Will New York City go to heaven? ... No, nature made us. Nature did it all, not the gods of the religions.

—*Thomas Edison*

There's an old saying that God exists in your search for him. I just want you to understand that I ain't looking.

—*Leslie Nielsen*

I'm so afraid of religion. Its capacity for murder is terrifying.
> —*Doris Lessing*

I prayed for freedom twenty years, but received no answer until I prayed with my legs.
> —*Frederick Douglass, former slave*

Technically, I'm an agnostic, but I definitely believe in hell—especially after watching the fall TV schedule.
> —*Matt Groening*

Of all learned men, the clergy show the lowest development of professional ethics. Any pastor is free to cadge customers from the divines of rival sects, and to denounce the divines themselves as theological quacks.

—*H. L. Mencken*

If God kills, lies, cheats, discriminates, and otherwise behaves in a manner that puts the Mafia to shame, that's okay, he's God. He can do whatever he wants. And anyone who adheres to this philosophy has had his sense of morality, decency, justice and humaneness warped beyond recognition by the very book that is supposedly preaching the opposite.

—*Dennis McKinsey*

If Woody Allen were a Muslim, he'd be dead
by now.
   —Salman Rushdie

I would never want to be a member of a group
whose symbol was a guy nailed to two pieces
of wood.
   —George Carlin

Believe nothing, no matter where you read it
or who said it, no matter if I have said it,
unless it agrees your own reason and your own
common sense.
   —Buddha

Maybe there is no actual place called Hell.
Maybe Hell is just having to listen to our
grandparents breathe through their noses when
they're eating sandwiches.
　　　—Jim Carrey

Intellectually, religious emotions are not creative
but conservative. They attach themselves readily to
the current view of the world and consecrate it.
　　　—John Dewey

Humanity's first sin was faith; the first virtue
was doubt.
　　　—Mike Huben

The Bible was a consolation to a fellow all alone in the old cell. The lovely thin paper with a bit of mattress coir [stuffing] in it, if you could get a match or a bit of tinder, was as good a smoke as ever I tasted.

—*Brendan Behan*

I'm strictly against people being allowed to declare a religious affiliation they are not even capable of spelling correctly.

—*David Kastrup*

An atheist is a man who has no invisible means of support.

—*John Buchan (also attributed to Aldous Huxley, Fulton J. Sheen, and others)*

No institution in modern civilization is so tyrannical and so unjust to woman as is the Christian Church. It demands everything from her and gives her nothing in return.

—Josephine K. Henry

Why should so much mental activity have stopped there, and not inquired what glory there was in an omnipotent being torturing forever a puny little creature who could in no way defend himself? Would it be to the glory of a man to fry ants.

—Charlotte Perkins Gilman

Dear friends—Man has created God; not God man.—Yours ever, Garibaldi

—Giuseppe Garibaldi

Toward no crime have men shown themselves so cold-bloodedly cruel as in punishing differences of belief.
—*James Russell Lowell*

We have our hands, we have our brains, we have the challenge all around us, and we have within (from whatever source) the will to strive. That is enough; there is no need to assert "belief" in that which we do not, as yet, know.
—*Robert A. Heinlein*

... go to church and chapel, you fools: listen to the parson, and shut your eyes, and open your mouths, and see what God will send you.
—*Robert Taylor*

The tragedy is that every brain cell devoted to belief in the supernatural is a brain cell one cannot use to make life richer or easier or happier.
—*Kay Nolte Smith*

There is no God.
But it does not matter.
Man is enough.
—*Edna St. Vincent Millay*

… faith and knowledge are related as the two scales of a balance; when the one goes up, the other goes down.
—*Arthur Schopenhauer*

Of all the animosities which have existed among mankind, those which are caused by difference of sentiments in religion appear to be the most inveterate and distressing, and ought most to be deprecated. I was in hopes, that the enlightened and liberal policy, which has marked the present age, would at least have reconciled *Christians* of every denomination so far, that we should never again see their religious disputes carried to such a pitch, as to endanger the peace of society.

—*George Washington*

… the vast mass of existing gods or divine persons, when we come to analyze them, do actually turn out to be dead and deified human beings…. I believe that corpse worship is the protoplasm of religion.

—*Grant Allen*

Soul is not even that Crackerjack prize that God and Satan scuffle over after the worms have all licked our bones. That's why, when we ponder— as sooner or later each of us must—exactly what we ought to be doing about our soul, religion is the wrong, if conventional, place to turn. Religion is little more than a transaction in which troubled people trade their souls for temporary and wholly illusionary psychological comfort—the old give-it-up-in-order-to-save-it routine. Religions lead us to believe that the soul is the ultimate family jewel and that in return for our mindless obedience; they can secure it for us in their vaults, or at least insure it against fire and theft. They are mistaken.
—*Tom Robbins*

How often in our house had I heard talk of superstitious idiots, often relatives, who hated a Satan they never knew and worshipped a God they didn't have the brains to doubt?
—*Tariq Ali*

When I am dead, I hope it may be said: "His sins were scarlet but his books were read."
—*Hillaire Belloc*

I have always been reasonably leery of religion because there are so many edicts in religion, "thou shalt not," or "thou shalt." I wanted my world of the future to be clear of that.
—*Gene Roddenberry*

When I was a kid, I used to pray every night for a new bicycle. Then I realized that the Lord doesn't work that way so I stole one and asked Him to forgive me.
—*Emo Phillips*

Gods are fragile things: they may be killed by a whiff of science or a dose of common sense.
—*Chapman Cohen*

Not one man in ten thousand has goodness of heart or strength of mind to be an atheist.
—*Samuel Taylor Coleridge*

Every time you understand something, religion becomes less likely. Only with the discovery of the double helix and the ensuing genetic revolution have we had grounds for thinking that the powers held traditionally to be the exclusive property of the gods might one day be ours.
—*Dr. James Watson*

The Universalists believe in a god which I do
not; but believe that their god, with all his moral
attributes ... is nothing more than a chimera of
their own imagination.
　　　　—*Abner Kneeland*

Ethiopians say that their gods are snub-nosed and
black, the Thracians that theirs have blue eyes and
red hair.
　　　　—*Xenophanes*

God is the only being who in order to reign does
not even need to exist.
　　　　—*Charles Baudelaire*

But tripping over all those churches wasn't the real problem. The real problem was all that time spent inside them, skipping over the facts of reality.
—*Sherry Matulis*

An apology for the devil—it must be remembered that we have only heard one side of the case. God has written all the books.
—*Samuel Butler*

If anyone ever tries to tell you that, for all its quirks and irrationality, religion is harmless or even beneficial for society, remember those 128 million Americans—and hundreds of millions more citizens of other nations—who might be helped by research that is being restricted by religious beliefs.
—*Peter Singer*

… if I declare National Prayer Day, then I've got to declare National No-Prayer Day for the atheists. They are American citizens too…. Nowhere is it mandated that we're the Christian States of America.
> —*Jesse Ventura*

The [Roman Catholic] Church being what she is cannot have the instincts of a gentleman.
> —*George E. Macdonald*

If God created us in His own image, we have more than returned him the favor.
> —*Voltaire*

The last superstition of the human mind is the superstition that religion in itself is a good thing, though it might be free from dogma. I believe, however, that the religious feeling, as feeling, is wrong, and the civilized man will have nothing to do with it…. [When the] shadow of religion disappeared forever … I felt that I was free from a disease.
—*Samuel Porter Putnam*

Heathen, *n.* A benighted creature who has the folly to worship something that he can see and feel.
—*Ambrose Bierce*

Religion is an illusion…
—*Sigmund Freud*

One of the proofs of the immortality of the soul is that myriads have believed in it. They have also believed the earth was flat.

  —*Mark Twain*

I'm not a person who feels very friendly toward organized religion. I think people have been brainwashed through the centuries. The churches, particularly the Catholic Church, are patriarchal organizations that have been invested with power for the sake of the people in power, who happen to be men. It breeds corruption. I found going to church every Sunday and on holy days an exercise in extreme boredom …

  —*Joyce Carol Oates*

I do not pretend to be able to prove that there is no God. I equally cannot prove that Satan is a fiction. The Christian God may exist; so may the Gods of Olympus, or of ancient Egypt, or of Babylon. But no one of these hypotheses is more probable than any other: they lie outside the region of even probable knowledge, and therefore there is no reason to consider any of them.

—*Bertrand Russell*

… truly religious people are resigned to everything, even to mediocre poetry….

—*Oscar Wilde*

… in our darkening world, religion is the poison in the blood. Where religion intervenes, mere innocence is no excuse. Yet we go on skating around this issue, speaking of religion in the fashionable language of "respect." What is there to respect in any of this, or in any of the crimes now being committed almost daily around the world in religion's dreaded name?
—*Salman Rushdie*

Say what you will about the Ten Commandments, you must always come back to the pleasant fact that there are only ten of them.
—*H. L. Mencken*

The Christian system of religion is an outrage on common sense. Why is man afraid to think?
—*Thomas Paine*

... we have the most religious freedom of any country in the world, including the freedom not to believe....
    —*Bill Clinton*

Despite the solace of hypocritical religiosity and its seductive promise of an after-life of heavenly bliss ... most of us will do anything to thwart the inevitable victory of biological death.
    —*Jack Kevorkian*

... miracles have no claim whatever to the character of historical facts and are wholly invalid as evidences of any revelation.
    —*John Stuart Mill*

The pioneers and missionaries of religion have
been the real cause of more trouble and war than
all other classes of mankind.
　　　—*Edgar Allan Poe*

One is often told that it is a very wrong thing
to attack religion, because religion makes men
virtuous. So I am told; I have not noticed it.
　　　—*Bertrand Russell*

At present there is not a single credible established
religion in the world.
　　　—*George Bernard Shaw*

The memory of my own suffering has prevented me from ever shadowing one young soul with any of the superstitions of the Christian religion.
—*Elizabeth Cady Stanton*

I'm an atheist, but I'm very relaxed about it. I don't preach my atheism, but I have a huge amount of respect for people like Richard Dawkins who do. Anything he does on television, I will watch. [Then my publicist says,] "… There we go, Dan, that's half of America that's not going to see the next Harry Potter film on the back of that comment."
—*Daniel Radcliffe*

As a historian, I confess to a certain amusement
when I hear the Judeo-Christian tradition praised
as the source of our concern for human rights.
In fact, the great religious ages were notable
for their indifference to human rights in the
contemporary sense.

—*Arthur Schlesinger, Jr.*

In the realm of science, all attempts to find any
evidence of supernatural beings, of metaphysical
conceptions, as God, immortality, infinity, etc.,
thus have failed, and if we are honest, we must
confess that in science there exists no God, no
immortality, no soul or mind as distinct from the
body, but scientifically God and immortality are
illogical conceptions….

—*Charles Proteus Steinmetz*

I don't know why some people change churches—
what difference does it make which one you stay
home from?
　　　—*Rev. Denny Brake*

The Christian ideal has not been tried and
found wanting. It has been found difficult; and
left untried.
　　　—*G. K. Chesterton*

The more I study religions the more I am
convinced that man never worshipped anything
but himself.
　　　—*Richard Francis Burton*

Going to church doesn't make you a Christian any more than going to a garage makes you a car.
—*Dr. Laurence J. Peter*

Thus the effectiveness of a doctrine should not be judged by its profundity, its sublimity or the validity of the truths it embodies, but by how thoroughly it insulates the individual from his self and the world as it is. What Pascal said of an effective religion is true of any effective doctrine: It must be "contrary to nature, to common sense, and to pleasure."
—*Eric Hoffer*

There once was a time when all people believed in God and the church ruled. This time was called the Dark Ages.
—*Richard Lederer*

The Bible is not the Word of God. If God exists,
I believe he would take less offense at my not
believing in his existence than to believe that he/
she performed the atrocities ascribed to him by the
authors of the Bible.
        —*Kyle Kelly*

If your Bible is an argument for the degradation
of woman, and the abuse by whipping of little
children, I advise you to put it away, and use your
common sense instead.
        —*Lucy Colman*

A Sunday school is a prison in which children do penance for the evil conscience of their parents.
—*H. L. Mencken*

The fact that a believer is happier than a skeptic is no more to the point than the fact that a drunken man is happier than a sober one.
—*George Bernard Shaw*

Acceptance without proof is the fundamental characteristic of Western religion. Rejection without proof is the fundamental characteristic of Western science.
—*Gary Zukav*

Few nations have been so poor as to have but one god. Gods were made so easily, and the raw material cost so little, that generally the god market was fairly glutted and heaven crammed with these phantoms.
>   —*Robert Ingersoll*

In our windy world, what's up is faith, what's down is heresy.
>   —*Alfred Tennyson*

A religion is a cult that succeeded.
>   —*Unknown*

When his life was ruined, his family killed, his farm destroyed, Job knelt down on the ground and yelled up to the heavens, "Why God? Why me?" and the thundering voice of God answered, "There's just something about you that pisses me off."
—*Stephen King*

I don't believe in an afterlife, although I am bringing a change of underwear.
—*Woody Allen*

Thanks be to God, I'm still an atheist.
—*Luis Buñuel*

Men are given to worship malevolent gods, and that which is not cruel seems to them not worth their adoration.
  —*Anatole France*

Christ died for our sins. Dare we make his martyrdom meaningless by not committing them?
  —*Jules Feiffer*

Religion, *n.* A daughter of Hope and Fear, explaining to Ignorance the nature of the Unknowable.
  —*Ambrose Bierce*

Three Good Arguments Jesus Was Black:
1. He called everyone "brother."
2. He liked gospel.
3. He couldn't get a fair trail.

Three Good Arguments Jesus Was from California:
1. He never cut his hair.
2. He walked around barefoot all the time.
3. He started a new religion.

Three Good Arguments Jesus Was Jewish:
1. He went into his father's business.
2. He lived at home until he was 33.
3. He was sure his mother was a virgin, and his mother was sure he was God.

    —Unknown

It's always better to tell the truth. The truth doesn't hurt, and saying that, my mother only ever lied to me about one thing. She said there was a God. But that's because when you're a working-class mum, Jesus is like an unpaid babysitter. She thought if I was God-fearing, then I'd be good.

—*Ricky Gervais*

You asked about the afterlife. Well, I can't take bets on it. Who's going to take my bet, you know? I, myself, don't believe in any afterlife. I do believe in this life, and what you do in this life is what it's all about.

—*Studs Terkel*

… if we must play the theological game, let us never forget that it is a game. Religion, it seems to me, can survive only as a consciously accepted system of make-believe.
—*Aldous Huxley*

The church has always been willing to swap off treasures in heaven for cash down.
—*Robert Ingersoll*

O Lord, please don't burn us.
Don't grill or toast your flock.
Don't put us on the barbecue,
Or simmer us in stock.
Don't braise or bake or boil us,
Or stir-fry us in a wok.
—*Graham Chapman (of Monty Python)*

Everything comes from neurotics. They alone have founded religions and composed our masterpieces.
—*Unknown*

If God had intended for us not to masturbate, he would've made our arms shorter.
—*George Carlin*

Human society is born in the shadow of religious fear, and in that stage the suppression of heresy is a sacred social duty. Then comes the rise of a priesthood, and the independent thinker is met with punishment in this world and the threat of eternal damnation hereafter…. Religion is the last thing man will civilize.
—*Chapman Cohen*

If Jesus came back and saw what's going on in his name, he'd never stop throwing up.
> —*Frederick in the movie* Hannah and
> Her Sisters

Once people get hung up on theology, they've lost sanity forever. More people have been killed in the name of Jesus Christ than any other name in the history of the world.
> —*Gore Vidal*

I am a deeply religious nonbeliever.... This is a somewhat new kind of religion.
> —*Albert Einstein*

… any system of religion, that has anything in it that shocks the mind of a child, cannot be a true system.

—*Thomas Paine*

"GOD" is most accurately defined as the personification of ignorance, representing everything that we do not yet understand.

—*Kenneth Marsalek*

Religion is a delusion propagated by a combination of ignorance, art, and fear, fanned into longevity and ubiquity by the power it gave those in command.

—*P. W. Atkins*

Perhaps our role on this planet is not to worship God—but to create him.
　　　—*Arthur C. Clarke*

Religion is an insult to human dignity. With or without it, you'd have good people doing good things and evil people doing evil things, but for the good people to do evil things, it takes religion.
　　　—*Steven Weinburg*

God was invented to explain mystery. God is always invented to explain those things that you do not understand.
　　　—*Richard Feynman*

... the press and the pulpit have in every age and every nation been on the side of the exploiting class and the ruling class.
> —*Eugene V. Debs*

I have found Christian dogma unintelligible. Early in life I absented myself from Christian assemblies.
> —*Benjamin Franklin*

I believe that religion, generally speaking, has been a curse to mankind.
> —*H. L. Mencken*

Religion … is the sign of the oppressed creature, the heart of a heartless world, and the soul of soulless conditions. It is the opium of the people.
 —*Karl Marx*

A Christian is a man who feels repentance on a Sunday for what he did on Saturday and is going to do on Monday.
 —*Thomas Ybarra*

Religion is a magic device for turning unanswerable questions into unquestionable answers.
 —*Art Gecko*

Well, you could become a Southern Baptist. I mean, instead of having to obey the Pope, you could just obey your husband.
—*Arianna Huffington*

The best cure for Christianity is reading the Bible.
—*Mark Twain*

Do you know the three times that most people are in church? When they are hatched, matched, and dispatched.
—*Lowell B. Yoder*

The best place to meditate is on the pot. If you have a comfortable toilet seat and a stout lock on the door, there's no telling what great thoughts might emerge. Martin Luther dreamed up Protestantism whilst sitting on the toilet at Wittenburg monastery, and we know what a big movement that became.
—*Anton LaVey*

Religion is to the brain what a tapeworm is to an intestine.
—*Unknown*

Religious belief is a mental illness. A very contagious one.
—*Unknown*

Just in terms of allocation of time resources, religion is not very efficient. There's a lot more I could be doing on a Sunday morning.
—*Bill Gates*

Believe those who are seeking truth, doubt those who find it.
—*André Gide*

Jesus never heard of Beethoven and Bach. Why aren't we playing more country music in church?
—*Tex Sample*

It is natural that people should differ most, and most violently, about the unknowable…. There is all the room in the world for divergence of opinion about something that, so far as we can realistically perceive, does not exist.

—*E. Haldeman-Julius*

Sure, I love fairy tales.

—*Maynard James Keenan's response when asked about whether or not he reads the Bible*

I always said a very short prayer to God; here it is: "My God! make my enemies very ridiculous." God heard my prayer.

—*Voltaire*

There's a Bible on that shelf there. But I keep it
next to Voltaire—poison and antidote.
  —Bertrand Russell

I would like—and this would be the last and most
ardent of my wishes—I would like the last of the
kings to be strangled by the guts of the last priest.
  —Jean Meslier

Hearing nuns' confessions is like being stoned to
death with popcorn.
  —Fulton J. Sheen

A good sermon should be like a woman's skirt: short enough to arouse interest, but long enough to cover all the essentials.

—*Ronald Knox*

I am not going to question your opinions. I am not going to meddle with your belief. I am not going to dictate to you mine. All that I say is, examine, inquire. Look into the nature of things. Search out the grounds of your opinions, the for and the against. Know why you believe, understand what you believe, and possess a reason for the faith that is in you.

—*Frances Wright*

Religion is a bandage that man has invented to protect a soul made bloody by circumstance.

—*Theodore Dreiser*

And of all Plagues with which Mankind are Curst,
Ecclesiastic Tyranny's the worst.
　　—*Daniel Defoe*

During almost fifteen centuries, has the legal
establishment of Christianity been on trial. What
have been its fruits? More or less, in all places,
pride and indolence in the clergy; ignorance and
servility in the laith; in both, superstition, bigotry
and persecution.
　　—*James Madison*

I sometimes think that God, in creating man,
somewhat overestimated his ability.
　　—*Oscar Wilde*

My Bible-thumping cousin once claimed that Jesus must have risen from the dead since thousands of people saw him after the resurrection. I simply pointed out that if that was the case then Elvis should be deified because thousands of people have seen him in McDonald's since 1977.
——*Rand Race*

Based on the number of 'tards who "find him," I suspect Jesus really sucks at hide-n-seek.
——*Marc Wolfe*

A fanatic is a man who does what he thinks the Lord would do if He knew the facts of the case.
——*Finley Peter Dunne*

If you're following the news, you know that the major religions differ in their interpretation of the holy books. For example, one way to interpret God's will is that you should love your neighbor. An alternate reading of the holy books might lead you to rig a donkey cart with small mortar rockets and aim it at a hotel full of infidels. In summary, po-tay-to, poh-tah-to. Religions are very flexible.

—*Scott Adams*

So many Gods, so many creeds,
So many paths that wind and wind,
While just the art of being kind
Is all the sad world needs.

—*Ella Wheeler Wilcox*

This would be the best of all possible worlds if
there were no religion in it.
—*John Adams*

Born again Christians are an even bigger pain the
second time around.
—*Herb Caen*

One man's idea of hell is to be forced to remain in
another man's idea of heaven.
—*Unknown*

Saint, *n.* A dead sinner, revised and edited.
    —*Ambrose Bierce*

History does not record anywhere at any time a
religion that has any rational basis. Religion is a
crutch for people not strong enough to stand up to
the unknown without help.
    —*Robert A. Heinlein*

The only thing that stops God from sending a
second flood is that the first one was useless.
    —*Nicolas Chamfort*

If God were suddenly condemned to live the life which He has inflicted on men, He would kill Himself.

—*Alexandre Dumas*

It seems to me that organized creeds are collections of words around a wish.

—*Zora Neale Hurston*

All that my work has shown is that you don't have to say that the way the universe began was the personal whim of God.

—*Stephen Hawking*

As my ancestors are free from slavery, I am free from the slavery of religion.
—*Butterfly McQueen*

Who burnt heretics? Who roasted or drowned millions of "witches"? Who built dungeons and filled them? Who brought forth cries of agony from honest men and women that rang to the tingling stars? Who burnt Bruno? Who spat filth over the graves of Paine and Voltaire? The answer is one word: Christians.
—*G. W. Foote*

If you're born again, do you have two belly buttons?
—*Unknown*

I am convinced now that children should not be subjected to the frightfulness of the Christian religion.... If the concept of a father who plots to have his own son put to death is presented to children as beautiful and as worthy of society's admiration, what types of human behavior can be presented to them as *reprehensible*?
　　　　—*Ruth Hurmence Green*

I believe that when I am dead, I am dead. I believe that with my death I am just as much obliterated as the last mosquito you and I squashed.
　　　　—*Jack London*

Do you tell me that the Bible is against our rights?
Then I say that our claims do not rest upon a book
written no one knows when, or by whom…. Book
and opinions, no matter from whom they came, if
they are in opposition to human rights, are nothing
but dead letters.
  —*Ernestine Rose*

We all ought to understand we're on our own.
Believing in Santa Claus doesn't do kids any harm
for a few years but it isn't smart to continue waiting
all their lives for him to come down the chimney
with something wonderful. Santa Claus and God
are cousins.
  —*Andy Rooney*

Our dream dashes itself against
the great mystery like a wasp
against a window pane.
Less merciful than man,
God never opens the window.
　　　—Jules Renard

The religions we call false were once true.
　　　—Ralph Waldo Emerson

One religion after another has accepted and
perpetuated man's original mistake in making a
private servant of the mother of the race.
　　　—Charlotte Perkins Gilman

God's merits are so transcendent that it is not surprising his faults should be in reasonable proportion.
— *Samuel Butler*

The God of the Christians is a father who is a great deal more concerned about his apples than he is about his children.
— *Denis Diderot*

Heaven can do whatever it likes without anybody being able to interfere with it, especially when it is raining.
—*Miguel de Cervantes*

They say that God is everywhere, and yet we always
think of Him as somewhat of a recluse.
—*Emily Dickinson*

God was satisfied with his own work, and that
is fatal.
—*Samuel Butler*

I believe that it is better to tell the truth than to
lie. I believe that it is better to be free than to be a
slave. And I believe that it is better to know than to
be ignorant.
—*H. L. Mencken*

There can be no Creator, simply because his grief at the fate of his creation would be inconceivable and unendurable.
—Elias Canetti

I have too much respect the idea of God to make it responsible for such an absurd world.
—Georges Duhamel

Many a long dispute among divines may be thus abridg'd: It is so. It is not so. It is so. It is not so.
—Benjamin Franklin

God made everything out of nothing, but the nothingness shows through.
　　　—*Paul Valéry*

Religious belief is a mental illness. A contagious one.
　　　—*Unknown*

To what excesses will men not go for the sake of a religion in which they believe so little and which they practice so imperfectly.
　　　—*Jean de La Bruyère*

If there is a God he surely must be disappointed in the current state of earth and her people.
　　—*Eric Coltrane*

As the caterpillar chooses the fairest leaves to lay her eggs on, so the priest lays his curse on the fairest joys.
　　—*William Blake*

When one person suffers from a delusion, it is called insanity. When many people suffer from a delusion, it is called Religion.
　　—*Robert M. Pirsig*

Christians talk as though goodness was their idea
but good behavior doesn't have any religious origin.
Our prisons are filled with the devout.
—*Andy Rooney*

… there is nothing, I think, so odious as the
whitewashed outside of a specious zeal; as
those downright imposters, those bigots whose
sacrilegious and deceitful grimaces impose on
others with impunity, and who trifle as they like
with all that mankind holds sacred … those men
who, seized with strange ardour, make use of the
next world to secure their fortune in this ….
—*Molière*

When a religion is good, I conceive that it will support itself; and when it cannot support itself, and God does not take care to support it, so that its professors are obliged to call for the help of the civil power, it is a sign, I apprehend, of it being a bad one.

—*Benjamin Franklin*

There is no argument worthy of the name that will justify the union of the Christian religion with the State. Every consideration of justice and equality forbids it. Every argument in favor of free Republican institutions is equally an argument in favor of a complete divorce of the State from the Church. History in warning tones tells us there can be no liberty without it. Justice demands it. Public safety requires it. He who opposes it is, whether he realizes it or not, an enemy of freedom.

—*Benjamin Underwood*

We must respect the other fellow's religion, but only in the sense and to the extent that we respect his theory that his wife is beautiful and his children smart.
—*H. L. Mencken*

The point of all these way-out examples is that they are disprovable ... [Bertrand] Russell's point is that the burden of proof rests with the believers, not the non-believers.
—*Richard Dawkins*

Pray, *v.* To ask that the laws of the universe be annulled in behalf of a single petitioner confessedly unworthy.
—*Ambrose Bierce*

The faith in which I was brought up assured me that I was better than other people; I was "saved," they were "damned." We were in a state of grace and the rest were "heathens" …. Our hymns were loaded with arrogance—self-congratulation on how cozy we were with the Almighty, and what a high opinion he had of us, what hell everybody else would catch come Judgment Day.

> —*Jubal in the novel* Stranger in a Strange Land

If Morality was Christianity, Socrates was the Saviour.

> —*William Blake*

Sacred cows make the tastiest hamburger.

> —*Abbie Hoffman*

Christianity, even if it calls itself the religion of love, must be hard and unloving to those who do not belong to it.
— *Sigmund Freud*

… the spirit of rationalism laughed the whole thing to scorn, and science gave mankind a more cheerful view of life.
— *Elizabeth Cady Stanton*

I will not swear to God because I don't believe in the conventional nonsense.
— *Marlon Brando*

When I look up at the starry heavens at night and reflect upon what is it that I really see there, I am constrained to say, "There is no God."
—*John Burroughs*

The abominable laws respecting [women in the Bible] … are a disgrace to civilization and English literature. Any family which permits such a volume to lie on their parlor-table ought to be ostracized by all respectable society.
—*Ella E. Gibson*

If the ignorance of nature gave birth to gods, a knowledge of nature is calculated to destroy them.
—*Percy Bysshe Shelley*

Seeing there are no signs, nor fruit of "religion," but in man only, there is no cause to doubt, but that the seed of "religion" is also only in man.
—*Sir Thomas Hobbes*

I have found some astonishing answers to my questioning as to God and religion in his book: absolutely nothing.
—*Peter Ilich Tchaikovsky*

Religion would thus be the universal obsessional neurosis of humanity; like the obsessional neurosis of children, it arose out of the Oedipus complex, out of relation to the father.
—*Sigmund Freud*

The first requisite for the happiness of the people
is the abolition of religion.
>   —*Karl Marx*

I say I have no religious beliefs. I certainly think
this life is all I have, all anybody has, and I usually
say it doesn't seem to me at all meaningful to ask
the purpose of life. What purpose does the life of a
spider have? If a spider doesn't have a purpose, why
should we?
>   —*G. A. Wells*

We all have daddy issues ... gods are selfish; they
only care about themselves.
>   —*Percy Jackson, talking about the Greek god*
>   *Poseidon in the movie* Percy Jackson and
>   The Olympians

For, if God is, he is necessarily the eternal, supreme, absolute master, and, if such a master exists, man is a slave; now if he is a slave, neither justice, nor equality, nor fraternity, nor prosperity are possible for him…. Therefore, if God existed, only in one way could he serve human liberty—by ceasing to exist.

  —*Mikhail Bakunin*

We are here because one odd group of fishes had a peculiar fin anatomy that could transform into legs for terrestrial creatures; because the earth never froze entirely during an ice age; because a small and tenuous species, arising in Africa a quarter of a million years ago, has managed, so far, to survive by hook and by crook. We may yearn for a "higher answer"—but none exists.

  —*Stephen J. Gould*

I think I could turn and live with animals, they're
    so placid and self-contain'd, …
They do not sweat and whine about their condition,
They do not lie awake in the dark and weep for
    their sins,
They do not make me sick discussing their duty to
    God,
Not one is dissatisfied, not one is demented with
    the mania of owning things,
Not one kneels to another, nor to his kind that lived
    thousands of years ago,
Not one is respectable or unhappy over the whole
    earth.
     —Walt Whitman

The impotence of God is infinite.
     —Anatole France

People who believe in a divine creator, trying to live their lives in obedience to his supposed wishes and in expectation of a supposed eternal reward, are victims of the greatest confidence trick of all time.
　　　—Barbara Smoker

The world can only be redeemed through action—movement—motion. Uncoerced, unbribed and unbought, humanity will move toward the light.
　　　—Alice Hubbard

I believe in God, only I spell it Nature.
　　　—Frank Lloyd Wright

'Twas only fear first in the world made gods.
> —*Ben Jonson*

Atheism rises above creeds and puts Humanity
   upon one plane.
There can be no "chosen people" in the Atheist
   philosophy.
There are no bended knees in Atheism;
No supplications, no prayers;
No sacrificial redemptions;
No "divine" revelations;
No washing in the blood of the lamb;
No crusades, no massacres, no holy wars;
No heaven, no hell, no purgatory;
No silly rewards and no vindictive punishments;
No christs, and no saviors;
No devils, no ghosts and no gods.
> —*Joseph Lewis*

There is no theory of a God, of an author of
Nature, of an origin of the Universe, which is not
utterly repugnant to my facilities….
—*Harriet Martineau*

We have lost religion, but we have gained
humanism.
—*Jean-Paul Sartre*

Man is the Religious Animal. He is the only
Religious Animal. He is the only animal that has
the True Religion—several of them. He is the only
animal that loves his neighbor as himself, and cuts
his throat if his theology isn't straight. He has made
a graveyard of the globe in trying his honest best to
smooth his brother's path to happiness and heaven.
—*Mark Twain*

I realized early on that it is detailed scientific knowledge which makes certain religious beliefs untenable. A knowledge of the true age of the earth and of the fossil record makes it impossible for any balanced intellect to believe in the literal truth of every part of the Bible in the way that fundamentalists do. And if some of the Bible is manifestly wrong, why should any of the rest of it be accepted automatically? … What could be more foolish than to base one's entire view of life on ideas that, however plausible at the time, now appear to be quite erroneous? And what would be more important than to find our true place in the universe by removing one by one these unfortunate vestiges of earlier beliefs?

—*Francis Crick*

When you once attribute effects to the will of a personal God, you have let in a lot of little gods and devils—then sprites, fairies, dryads, naiads, witches, ghosts and goblins, for your imagination is reeling, riotous, drunk, afloat on the flotsam of superstition. What you know then doesn't count. You just believe, and the more you believe the more do you plume yourself that fear and faith are superior to science and seeing.
>   —*Elbert Hubbard*

Men of simple understanding, little inquisitive and little instructed, make good Christians.
>   —*Michel de Montaigne*

All knowledge that is not the real product of observation, or of consequences deduced from observation, is entirely groundless and illusory.
—*Jean Baptiste LaMarck*

Backward and forward, eternity is the same; already we have been the nothing we dread to be.
—*Herman Melville*

You have to be very religious to change your religion.
—*Comtesse Diane*

Religions are kept alive by heresies, which are really sudden explosions of faith.
> —*Gerald Brenan*

All religions will pass, but this will remain the same: simply sitting in a chair and looking into the distance.
> —*V. V. Rozanov*

It is, I think, an error to believe that there is any need of religion to make life seem worth living.
> —*Sinclair Lewis*

I lead a perfectly healthy, satisfactory life without being religious. And I think more people should try it.

—*Peter Watson*

When I told the people of Northern Ireland that I was an atheist, a woman in the audience stood up and said, "Yes, but is it the God of the Catholics or the God of the Protestants in whom you don't believe?"

—*Quentin Crisp*

I am an atheist (or at best a Unitarian who winds up in churches quite a lot).

—*Kurt Vonnegut*

Being an atheist is a matter not of moral choice,
but of human obligation.
—*John Fowles*

When the whole world doesn't believe in God, it'll
be a great place.
—*Philip Roth*

I don't have any faith, but I have a lot of hope, and
I have a lot of dreams of what we could do with our
intelligence if we had the will and the leadership
and the understanding of how we could take all
of our intelligence and our resources and create a
world for our kids that is hopeful.
—*Ann Druyan*

We [my family] are the kind of people…whatever our distant ancestors' religions—who do not believe, who do not carry on traditions….In my parents' general view, new things were better than old, and the very fact that some ritual had been performed in the past was a good reason for abandoning it now. Because what was the past, as our forebears knew it? Nothing but poverty, superstition and grief. "Think for yourself," Dad used to say. "Always ask why."
—*Barbara Ehrenreich*

We cannot be top country if we let science and education be run by people who think the dinosaurs drowned in Noah's flood.
—*Katha Pollitt*

…the being cannot be termed rational or virtuous who obeys any authority but that of reason.
—*Mary Wollstonecraft*

I have to admit that one of my favorite fantasies is that next Sunday not one single woman, in any country of the world, will go to church. If women simply stop giving our time and energy to the institutions that oppress, they would have to cease to do so.
—*Sonia Johnson*

From my point of view, I would ban religion completely….But the reality is that organized religion doesn't seem to work. It turns people into hateful lemmings and it's not really compassionate.
—*Elton John*

Wandering in a vast forest at night, I have only a faint light to guide me. A stranger appears and says to me: "My friend, you should blow out your candle in order to find your way more clearly." This stranger is a theologian.
—*Denis Diderot*

…Religion has been compelled by Science to give up one after another of its dogmas—of those assumed cognitions which it could not substantiate.
—*Herbert Spencer*

Science is the great antidote to the poison of enthusiasm and superstition.
—*Adam Smith*

The man who has no mind of his own lends it to the priests.
> —*George Meredith*

Properly read, the Bible is the most potent force for atheism ever conceived.
> —*Isaac Asimov*

Today, the theory of evolution is an accepted fact for everyone but a fundamentalist minority, whose objections are based not on reasoning but on doctrinaire adherence to religious principles.
> —*Dr. James Watson*

Index